Teaching on Your Own Terms

Teaching on Your Own Terms

The 5 Steps to Building the Online Teaching Business of Your Dreams

Elliot Phillips

Published by Game Changer Publishing

Paperback ISBN: 979-8-9856579-1-3
Hardcover ISBN: 979-8-9877531-2-5
Digital: ISBN: 979-8-9877531-3-2

www.GameChangerPublishing.com

DEDICATION

This book is dedicated to all of the teachers I've worked with that were brave enough to take that leap to be in control of their own futures.

ACCESS YOUR FREE GIFTS

Read This First

Just to say thanks for buying and reading my book, I would like to give you a few free bonus gifts, no strings attached!

To Download Your Free Gifts Now, Visit:

www.TeachOnYourOwnTerms.com/BookGifts

TESTIMONIALS

"The Ferrari of Tutoring Business Coaching" - **Abdullah Williams, English Tutor**

"If you are a teacher, YOU NEED TO READ THIS! I knew that I was a great teacher and loved helping children but I was burning out. I saw Elliot's ad one day and joined the Students on Demand program and my entire life changed!" - **Quanita Joseph, Reading Tutor**

"Elliot and his team are experts when it comes to exponentially growing a tutoring business." - **Arif Mohid, Aim High Tuition**

"I shifted my perspective from simply a tutor to a business owner. I learned how to speak to my clients in a way that made them absolutely jump at the chance to work with us. I have improved my delivery, my organic marketing strategy and my entire sales process. In the first 3 months of 2022, I exceeded my entire annual revenue of 2021!" - **Doulton Wiltshire, Finance Tutor**

"The program is gold. It requires a lot of work, but anything worth having does. What I have learnt is priceless. The shift in my mindset to be a business owner has probably had the most impact on me. I get to teach students how I want to and am impacting more kids' lives - which as a teacher - was my mission." - **Becca Louise, Client**

"I knew I needed help, not only to replace my income but also to continue doing what I love—working with student writers. Now that I followed the process for building a sustainable, scalable tutoring business, I'm working with real students in these programs I created exactly the way I wanted to. It's literally like watching my dreams come true, and I can't believe the possibilities ahead." - **Ashley Johnson Wood, Client**

"Elliot took me from never having earned a single penny through marketing my own services to regularly making £25k/month, and with a realistic goal of £100k/month before long. Worth ten times the investment!" - **Jacob Williams, English Tutor**

Teaching on Your Own Terms

The 5 Steps to Building the Online Teaching Business of Your Dreams

Elliot Phillips

www.GameChangerPublishing.com

Foreword

I have known Elliot Phillips for a number of years, and have watched his entrepreneurial journey unfold with admiration. When the pandemic struck and all the schools shut down, he launched The Teacher Project with impressive dynamism, and the results since then have been remarkable. He has helped many school teachers in a number of countries become highly successful online tutors, satisfying the booming demand for homeschooling.

More and more parents want to obtain extra learning help for their children. This book explains the best way to build a business to meet that need. Elliot understands the field because he is a former PE teacher from a family of teachers. He has taught in various schools and has also built an online business from scratch. His advice about how to market is invaluable – from developing leads to using paid advertising on social media.

He knows how teachers can find student clients and deliver great education and habits to those students so that they become committed customers. He understands that tutoring involves selling to both parents and their children. He explains how group tutoring is the absolute key to creating a highly profitable enterprise. He writes about the importance of developing a student community, and how the best tutors nurture their students.

This book is a highly specialist text – it shows how teachers can gain freedom and independence by starting their own business in online tutoring. It also helps prepare the reader mentally for the task ahead – Elliot talks about the mental models and self discipline a would-be entrepreneur needs to adopt in order to achieve great things.

Because of the turmoil of school closures and the ubiquity of Zoom and Teams as forms of communication, now is the best time ever to found a digital only tutoring business. This book will show you how it's done, by someone who has taught hundreds of tutors. I strongly recommend it to anyone who wants to start or scale an online tutoring business.

Good luck to all the tutor entrepreneurs out there!

Best
Luke Johnson

Table of Contents

Introduction 1

Chapter 1 – The Five to Thrive 13

Chapter 2 – Creating Your Signature Tutoring Offer 21

Chapter 3 – The Student Lead Machine 29

Chapter 4 – The Student Acquisition System 37

Chapter 5 – The Grand Slam Group Offer 47

Chapter 6 – The Scalable Delivery System 57

Conclusion 65

Introduction

T here's never been a better time to be a teacher. We're currently living in the golden age, or the golden era for educators & teachers who want to build the future generations of our students and our kids.

The pandemic threw schools into turmoil. Students didn't know if their exams were taking place or when they would be allowed to return to school. But there was one blessing in disguise—online learning. More and more teachers started to realize that they could teach from home and have a schedule that allowed them to control when they worked and how they worked, and they could work with students they actually wanted to work with.

After the pandemic, we started to see the private tutoring space explode. In fact, the industry is expected to grow to $276 billion by the year 2025. But not only this, education is changing for more than one reason. Education is changing because studies have also shown that 44% of teachers are expected to quit the profession by 2027, which ultimately means that there will be students who aren't given the education they deserve or are entitled to in schools. These numbers are from a study by the National Education Union in the United Kingdom. Another article from Changing America showed in 2022 that nearly two million fewer students enrolled in public schools. We started to see a trend. Teachers realized that they didn't have to commit to the classroom and trade their time for money doing a job they loved and were super passionate about while their own mental health and well-being suffered. They could teach from home. Not only did the teachers realize that, but the students and the parents also discovered the kids could be educated outside of school without the parents having to worry about sending their children to a school environment with students who perhaps didn't want to be there or who were having a negative impact, or the worry that teachers were suffering.

Ultimately, while it's not the teacher's fault, our students become a reflection of their teachers. So if the teachers are suffering, if the teachers are struggling because of the demands of the job, because of the red tape, because of all of the uncertainty and impossible schedule that they're expected to follow, it's naturally going to affect the students. Something had to change. We live in this window of opportunity where not only can the students thrive by getting access to better education outside of school, but the teachers now have this opportunity to put themselves on the map and start earning doctor and lawyer money and actually get paid what they truly deserve for making a massive contribution to society.

Teachers are responsible for building our future generations; without them, the world simply won't evolve. So in this book, I'm going to share how to seize this opportunity like many teachers are already doing.

Here's who this book is for. This book is for educators and teachers who have a passion for helping students reach their academic potential. Students who want to go on and evolve potentially into our next tech geniuses, into the people that make the world go round. This book is for teachers who want to actually start getting paid what they deserve because they know they have something special to give. So if you're an educator, this book is for you.

It's also for you if you're a teacher who's already started to tap into the power of online learning and has already started to build your online teaching business, but you're looking for ways to accelerate things faster. You're looking for ways to get in front of your ideal students and build a business that can scale: you're not trading time for money or stuck in Zoom jail while delivering one-on-one lessons every day. Because if you were to do that, it'd probably be safer and easier to stay in the classroom because that's simply more secure.

When you build your own business, the goal is to use your time smarter and earn money smarter. Let me give you some insight into who I am and why I'm qualified to write this book and speak to you about this topic.

But before I do that, here's what you're going to achieve by the end of the book. Once you go through this, there are a few things that you're going to learn. You're going to learn how to build a teaching business online where you can get your ideal students coming to you and not your competition. I will show you exactly how to fill your inbox with unlimited inquiries from students you love teaching, using predictable advertising strategies that I've taught to more than 500 teachers at the time of me writing this book. I'm also going to teach you how to build trust with students and parents so that by the time you speak to these parents and students interested in your services, you've built enough trust with them and you've managed to demonstrate value. You've shown them how you can help them so that the selling is done upfront. Then I'll share exactly how to convert students online into paying clients specifically for group tutoring so you have a business that can scale without having to trade your time for money teaching one-on-one. And then, I'll share with you how to create life-changing results for your students in a group environment using my six key delivery principles for group tutoring so that you can impact more students and scale your revenue without scaling your workload.

So who am I? My name is Elliot Phillips. I'm a former PE teacher. I left teaching back in July of 2015, and I have not only taught, but teaching lives and breathes in my own family. My mother is a teacher. She still teaches. My grandfather, my mother's dad, was a French teacher in schools across the UK and also abroad. That kind of set me on my way to wanting to be like my mom and grandfather because I liked giving—it runs in my blood. So once I left school, as I was very into sports, I paired the two together, and I had the goal of becoming a PE teacher.

My first role after I graduated from both college and university with a degree in sports performance was with a company that partnered with local schools around Northamptonshire, where I grew up, to deliver the national PE curriculum and also to train the teachers at these schools to deliver better PE lessons for students.

I met my wife in 2012 and decided to move to London to begin a new chapter. Luckily, I had earned my degree, so I quickly found a job teaching in a school in East London. So off I went. I continued teaching for two more years until July 2015, when it had got to the point where I realized that no matter how much I enjoyed working with students and teaching them, it was not going to allow me to create the life I wanted for my wife and our future family. There were times when I would finish at school, pick up the groceries on the way back home across London, and I'd have to scan things back through the checkouts. I'd be standing there bright red, completely embarrassed because I didn't have the money to pay for all the items. I lived in London, but hadn't really been out of my flat because what I was getting paid working as a teacher barely allowed me to pay the bills, and every month I was drowning in debt—life wasn't fun.

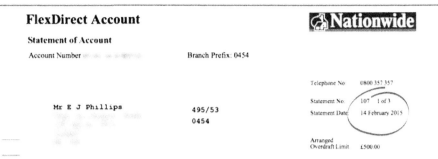

FlexDirect Account

Statement of Account

Account Number   Branch Prefix: 0454

Telephone No	0800 357 357
Statement No.	107 1 of 3
Statement Date	14 February 2015

Mr E J Phillips   495/53
                       0454

Arranged
Overdraft Limit   £500.00

IBAN: GB14 NAIA 0701 1641 8251 21 BIC: NAIAGB21 SWIFT INTERMEDIARY BANK: MIDLGB22

Date	Details	Payments	Receipts	Balance
2015				-443.98
15 Jan				
				-511.45
16 Jan			200.00	
			110.00	
				-465.77
19 Jan				-485.81
20 Jan				-499.81
21 Jan			1,514.94	
				1,007.58
22 Jan				
			34.05	659.33
23 Jan				
				538.78
24 Jan				512.91
26 Jan			50.00	
				462.91

My wife and I hadn't been on a romantic date in about two years. Our dates consisted of me picking up ready meals from the supermarket and cooking them at home. I wanted more, and I knew I deserved more. Then there were the early starts, traveling across London, taking school sports teams to games or matches after-school, waiting for students to get picked up after those games or matches, parents being late, then going to the gym on the way home, it would be after 8 p.m. sometimes by the time I arrived at home. I was stuck on a hamster wheel of "teach-eat-sleep-repeat."

To top it off, at the time, my wife worked nights, so there were many times when we'd kiss in the hallway as she went out the door when I arrived back, and that would be it. It kind of felt like, although we lived together, we only saw each other on the weekends.

I decided enough was enough.

At this point, I had spent every spare second I had in my day trying to build various online businesses because I just knew I needed to do something different. I tried to build a nutrition supplement company and a clothing company during my lunch breaks at school in the staffroom. Moving to London was a huge wake-up call for me. I could smell the hunger in the air, I could feel the success, motivation, and energy of the city, and it was literally a case of sink or swim. London allowed the entrepreneurial blood I had running through my veins to flow so I could swim, and for that, the city has a special place in my heart.

I knew if I could find something online, it would give me unlimited possibilities. I wanted to travel outside of the school holidays, and I knew if I could develop a business or learn how to work online, I'd be able to travel when I wanted, how I wanted, and work from anywhere in the world. And that was a goal of mine and my wife's.

So, once I left teaching, I had already gained some experience in trying to set these businesses up. I experienced failure because I didn't have anybody to help and guide me back then. I spent every second trying to figure things out on my own, and that learning curve helped me develop a "do not quit" work ethic. I can honestly say this has been critical to helping get me to where I am now. So while I didn't get very far from my first few shots at building my own business, I picked up a few skill sets that would benefit me later, which I'll talk to you about later in the book.

Now, the first thing I did after I left teaching in East London was a natural switch to become a personal trainer because physical well-being and teaching fitness went hand in hand with teaching PE. I saw it as an opportunity to connect with people in London whom I could build strong relationships with and learn from. Ultimately that's what happened. So I spent the next two years, until 2017, personal training. And I began to develop a great friendship with one of my clients who was a very successful entrepreneur.

I remember Christmas of 2016, he bought a book that changed everything! Little did I know that after reading the book, I would hire my first mentor. That mentor taught me how to work smarter inside my fitness business. I started working with clients in London, not in a one-on-one environment, but in a small group environment. My mentor taught me how to build communities and charge more for small group personal training per client than I was charging clients previously for one-on-one training sessions.

In the end, I was earning about five times more in an hour than normal personal trainers in London. I'd learned how to work smarter, not harder. Things really took off! It got to the point where people would walk past group coaching sessions in the parks and see how effective my sessions with my clients were, and they'd inquire about becoming a client too. I'd end up taking more and more clients on and launching new group sessions to cater to the increase in demand.

But I still lacked the knowledge of how to hire, develop, and move the business forward. So I ended up back in the position of trading my time for money again, even when I was personal training.

Then came the birth of my first daughter in May 2017. After she was born, unfortunately, she became extremely ill, and we spent the next two months in Great Ormond Street Hospital in London. This caused an abrupt halt to the growth of my training business, and I stopped taking on new clients. I even had to let a lot of them go because my time needed to be spent at the hospital supporting my wife and making sure I was the rock for the family during this difficult time.

It also meant that I was able to spend a lot of time on my laptop. So I started to look at how I could do personal training online, and from this point forward (May to December 2017), I worked relentlessly to build my business online just like I tried previously with the failed nutrition and clothing companies when I was teaching. I spent months building out the perfect program to launch my fitness business online. And when it came time to launch, I failed again—I'll explain.

This time it was a little more serious. My wife was no longer working as she was caring for our daughter, so I was responsible for providing for the entire family. I had spent almost everything I was earning from my personal training business on social media advertising campaigns to get my online fitness business off the ground, and I didn't get a single client. Desperate like a gambler in a casino, I continued spending all my money on marketing, believing my fortunes had to change—still nothing. I was close to landing our family in big trouble if things didn't take a turn for the better.

I couldn't figure out the puzzle of why I couldn't get clients even though what I had created was amazing. I knew if I could get clients, I could help them because my product was fantastic. So I swallowed my pride and booked a call with a coach I had been watching online for a few months. I was about to get served a butt-kicking. I remember having a conversation with him on a Friday night, and after the call, I walked into the living room, and my wife said, "What the hell has just happened to you? You're bright red." On the call, this coach told me exactly what all of the mistakes I had been making were, what I should be doing, and what was going to happen if I didn't decide to make a big change. I knew he was right.

Embarrassingly, I had just over $100 in my bank account that I could use without tapping into the next month's rent money because I'd blown everything on my failed online business ventures again. So there was no way I could invest and work with this person. The investment to get this coach's help was $6,000, and I knew I had to find a way to move forward because I couldn't keep doing what I was doing. Even though I was earning enough money to support our family in London with my personal training, I was addicted to spending it all on social media advertising to finally get my online business off the ground and I was probably only one failed campaign away from not being able to pay the rent. So everything was on the line.

After some intense conversations with my parents, they reluctantly lent me the money to work with this coach, and things transformed quickly. He immediately showed me why I was failing and how to identify who my ideal clients were. Within the first month of launching my online fitness business with this coach, I enrolled 156 clients and finally cracked the code. I'd finally discovered how to bring in clients who I wanted to work with on demand.

So I launched my business, the Teacher Fit Project, where I worked specifically with teachers who wanted to become more productive, have more energy, and wanted to improve their mental well-being and mental health so that they could show up better for their students and build a better work-life balance for themselves by working smarter and learning how to plan more effectively. It was a huge success. Within the next 18 months, my coach asked me to become the business strategist for his clients.

I ended up working and managing a batch of around 250 clients, helping them build their online fitness businesses from the ground up. This allowed me to work very closely with this mentor, who helped me finally gain the skill sets that I needed to get my own online business off the ground and scale it. It allowed me to see how a multimillion-dollar business ran behind the scenes. I picked up a lot of knowledge, and in 2019, at a conference in San Francisco, I had the "aha" moment.

I had gone from teaching in a school to taking my business online and working with other professionals to help them build and scale their own online businesses and doing it remotely while traveling to places like Bali, the Philippines, Los Angeles, and New York. There's no reason why I can't help the math teachers, the science teachers, the English teachers, the same teachers that used to tell me in the staff room they were tired and looking forward to the next school holiday even though it was the start of the school term. So I had the "aha" moment, and I spent the rest of 2019 mapping out exactly how I was going to help these teachers take their expertise online and build the life they wanted, that they deserved, and get paid what they deserved.

But there was a problem. I had imposter syndrome that there wouldn't be any teachers who would want to buy from me, that this wasn't something that these teachers wanted, and it would be a failure. So, I didn't press the go button. Then the pandemic hit, and the whole world turned upside down overnight. I remember on a Thursday evening watching the UK Prime Minister at the time, Boris Johnson, announce on national TV that every single school in the country was closing its doors and the country was going into lockdown.

The entire country was locked down, and that was the push I needed to press that Go button. And because I'd learned how to advertise effectively to get clients in my current online business, I knew exactly how to do this very fast, very quickly. I launched my first advertisements for the teachers the very next day after Boris Johnson's announcement. Within 24 hours, I had teachers booking to speak with me at an overwhelming pace. Before long, my calendar was full.

It was crazy. There I was, speaking with teachers daily, enrolling them into my first "beta" program for online tutors. The first thing I knew I needed to do was validate that my methods would actually work for teachers to build their own businesses online. So I started working with 50 teachers exclusively for the next twelve weeks. During that time, I walked them through all the steps I had created, showing them exactly how to identify their ideal students, market their business, and implement all of the advertising skills that I'd learned through all of my failures and working with my previous coaches. I then added the methods I'd developed along the way.

As I expected, these teachers started to see incredible results. Their calendars were booked full with students wanting to work with them. Since then, over the last few years, we've been fortunate enough to go from a business at ground zero to the end of 2022, generating revenue of $3 million and helping more than 500 teachers. And many of the success stories we've created for teachers are life-changing. I'm going to share some of their success stories in the following chapters.

So that's enough about me. Let's have a look at how you, the teacher, the educator, can take your passion online and get your expertise into the hands of the students who need it in a way that means you can work less, earn more, get paid what you deserve, and have more impact on today's students. This is why there's never been a better opportunity to be a teacher. I'm going to share with you exactly how to do things the right way to build your own online teaching business.

Chapter One

The Five to Thrive

While working with teachers in my first successful online business, the Teacher Fit Project, one of the things we worked on was building a routine that actually set you up for success. This is a routine that I developed while I was teaching back in school to ensure that although I was working long hours, I still had the energy to get me through the day. And of course, being the PE teacher and being involved in sports, I already naturally had a little bit more energy or "get up and go."

After I shared it with the teachers I was working with in the Teacher Fit Project, something incredible happened. My clients started to get to the end of the school day and found they had a second wind. They started to get more work done. These teachers were becoming more energized at school. And as a result, they were able to pour into the students and help the students to a greater level. Not only that, they experienced the benefits of feeling fitter and healthier.

When I launched the Teacher Project, working with the tutors, I taught them this same routine before they could do anything else. Before we talked about any business principles, I explained you can't build a house on a foundation of sand. I knew that having the right mindset, the right routines, and the ability to produce work faster would be key to their success.

I knew that they needed to be able to work smarter, not harder. I knew that they needed to have more energy to implement all of the business strategies I was about to teach them. There's a quote I once read that goes something like, "High income can only be generated by a high energy source." Many of them were skeptical at first, but they sure thanked me later. I'm going to walk you through each of the stages in what I now call the *Five to Thrive*: Five simple rituals, habits, whatever you want to call them, that will set you up for success inside of your business.

Whether you're a teacher who is already healthy, productive and you already work smarter, not harder, there's going to be something in these pages that can help you hit the next level. And if you're a teacher who doesn't yet have great routines, doesn't prioritize themselves, or feels like you're at the bottom of the pile, each one of these *Five to Thrive* principles will help you too. We're going to walk through exactly what they are because the goal here is to become the business owner, not just the teacher. If you continue being just a teacher, you will not be able to make smart decisions inside of your business.

While being a great teacher *is* required to teach online and help your students win, you must help yourself win first because you can't pour from an empty cup. Let's walk through the first one of my *Five to Thrive* principles.

The first one is called the **Morning Mind Reset**. I did this little routine every morning as soon as I woke up. Now, this might sound simple, but it's important, especially if you are a teacher and particularly if you are running a business or trying to build your business, because everybody experiences stress, and everybody feels tired at some point. How you start the day is quite often how you end the day. If you take any negative energy from the previous day into the new day, then there's a high chance that you'll experience the same outcome.

For example, if a student's behavior made you go home that evening and worry or fear going to the next lesson with that student. Or suppose you've already started your online teaching business, and you're already working with students, yet you're tired and fed up, or you're struggling to retain the students you teach. In that case, it just doesn't feel like anything's working, which can be a huge burden on you mentally. No matter how hard things get, you have to start every day positively. And when you do that, you start to focus on what's good, not on what's bad.

This is important because what we focus on, we attract, and what we focus on, we're more likely to achieve. So I developed this Morning Mind Reset routine where I run through a few things like gratitude, focusing on what I was grateful for, whether it was something big or something small. Maybe it was the smile on my daughter's face or that I had a roof over my head, it didn't matter. I looked for the positives. Then I would focus on my goals, what I wanted to achieve, why I wanted to accomplish these goals, and what it felt like when I achieved them.

Truthfully, this is what kept me going through all of the difficult times I mentioned at the start of this book. It was my vision for my business because business isn't easy. And that's why most people fail, because they think it's going to be easy. They think it's a sprint, but it's actually a marathon. So realigning myself with the vision of where I was taking my business each and every day: The teachers that I wanted to help, the lives I was going to change, and the students' lives that they were going to change. Focusing on that every single day reminded me of why I had to have energy today, of why I had to move forwards and not focus on what had happened the previous day. So I started every single day with a fresh outlook.

The last thing I did was I empowered myself with positive affirmations to become the leader that I needed to be. Remember, your clients will only grow to the level of their leader. Clients will never outgrow their leader. I had to make sure that I was continually growing myself. I had to help myself and remind myself who I was and who I needed to become. And it's the same for you as the teacher. If you're at a point where you're tired of your job and know that you're capable of more, but you don't believe that you can do it, you don't believe in yourself, then nobody else is going to believe in you. You have to step forward first. The first thing you need to do every morning is to put yourself in a powerful state so you can have energy. Because, as I said, only high energy can produce high income.

So that was the first thing, the Morning Mind Reset. The second thing I call **Plan Like a Producer**. This was something that I taught to the teachers back when I was running the Teacher Fit Project. I knew that their workload was very demanding. I knew that they would have a pile of books to go home and mark every day, plan the next day's lessons and at the same time have a never ending "to-do" list.

What happened when these teachers created to-do lists to try and fit themselves into their own schedules was that they would end up doing everything on these lists that was easy first because our brain is wired to do what's easy and comfortable. So the teachers' big goals and big ideas never got accomplished or achieved because they would shave off the quick, simple, easy tasks. They were busy being busy.

So I developed my producer routine. We mapped out three to five big goals, big ideas of what the teachers wanted to accomplish and wanted to achieve every semester or school term. Then we created a goal dump where we put everything else on the sheet of paper that they also wanted to achieve—sort of like what you probably have as your to-do list. We made sure first that we had the rocks. And you've probably heard the story about the rocks and the sand, where if you had a jar and put the sand in first, the rocks ultimately wouldn't fit into the jar. But if you put the rocks in first, the sand can go in between the cracks, and you can fit everything in the jar. This is that. But we took it a step further.

Once we had everything down on a piece of paper, we would then prioritize each of these goals, each of these big rocks, and even all of the little goals we'd categorize from A to Z. Then, every day, we only put the first letter onto the page of the journal, planner, or diary that needed to get done. You only put down the first letter on the sheet so that we could tackle the big tasks first, and because what you see, you'll do; what you see, you pay attention to. We forgot about everything else. Nothing else was allowed to go in your journal, diary, or planner until that big rock was checked off.

Once the rock that had been graded priority "A" was complete, priority "B" was allowed to go onto the journal or the planner. This worked wonders for the teachers that I was working with. In fact, at one point, a lot of them would find that just by operating like this, they would ultimately end up having an extra day a week in additional time. And it's the same with growing your business. You have to become a better producer. You have to learn how to get done what's important first because business is fast. You need to be able to move quickly, and you need to avoid being overwhelmed. You need to become the business owner who produces things fast.

One of the key traits I have developed over the years is condensing time from reaching a decision—to implementing—to completion. I taught this to my clients so they could get a lot more work done, even if it felt like they had none. So if a teacher wanted to build their business online while they were still working in the classroom, I could coach them to become a better producer, so they could stay on top of the workload and build their business simultaneously.

The next component of my *Five to Thrive* routine is **Building Your Engine**. Think of it like this: My first car was a Ford Fiesta. It wasn't a particularly fast car. In fact, the Ford Fiesta is pretty slow. At the time, it was a good car for me, but when I was driving on the highway, other cars would overtake me with minimal effort. Imagine a Ferrari up against a Ford Fiesta in a race. Which car is going to win? The Ferrari driver, of course, not because they're a better driver, but because their car has a bigger engine and it's more powerful. It's a beast compared to the small, slow Ford Fiesta. They get to where they want to go quicker and sooner.

So I asked myself, *How could I become like this? How could my clients become like this and operate like this? How could they get more done in less time without just having to rely on just planning?* And the answer was optimizing their body. The stronger they became, the more energy they would develop. The more muscle they could build, the more powerful they became. So we built out a routine where we focused on becoming physically fitter. We focused on our well-being, not to look strong, not to look ripped, but to build the engine that would allow us to become quicker in our decision-making, have more energy, and ultimately become the Ferrari.

The next step was to **Fuel Your Engine** to ensure that the Ferrari could keep operating at the same speed. It needs fuel consistently, and it needs the right fuel. You wouldn't put the wrong fuel source, gasoline or petrol, into your car because if you do, it will break down. This leads me to another big problem: The food teachers would eat and how they fueled themselves in the classroom, no wonder they had no energy. They weren't consuming the right fuel sources that helped their bodies function optimally. What they were putting in their body, of course, was making them crash. It wasn't giving them the energy or support they needed to even make it through the school day, which then contributed to them feeling more tired and having poor sleeping patterns.

Having come from the personal training world after teaching in 2015, I gained a lot of knowledge and expertise about how to fuel your body correctly. So I taught the teachers exactly how to fuel themselves (what to eat, when to eat) so that they didn't have to feel low on energy. They could actually develop a body that functions like a Ferrari, and they became faster and naturally felt better.

At the end of the day, health is wealth. So I developed this routine that allowed the teachers I worked with to feel like they were on top of the world. They had the foundation in place to go ahead and build the business of their dreams. But there was one more thing left. One more problem needed to be solved, and without this, the *Five to Thrive* doesn't work.

Tracking Targets. The issue was that some people wouldn't stay accountable to this routine, even though they knew it was important and felt the benefits. I started to see some of my clients fall off the wagon because they were still trained to do what was easy or they didn't like change when things got hard. The only way to stay accountable is to track what you're doing. If you don't set a target or track yourself toward that target, then you'll never be able to see progress. As renowned entrepreneur Tony Robbins says, "Progress equals happiness." So, I developed a tracking routine so the teachers could hold themselves accountable and see how much they were progressing, so they stayed motivated.

It's the same for our students. If we don't track our students' progress in school, how will we ever be able to complete their reports? How will we ever see the difference in our students' learning if we don't monitor how they're doing and how they're progressing and keep them accountable? So the same matters for us.

The same is true for whatever you're doing, whether enrolling students or advertising to grow your business, which we'll discuss later in the book. The same is important for you and your routines. If you want to have the perfect foundations in place and you want to have the launch pad to become the business owner, not just the teacher, you need to be able to track your habits.

Chapter Two

Creating Your Signature Tutoring Offer

In this chapter, I will introduce to you something I call the *Rule of One*. The first issue I noticed back when I started planning my program to help teachers build their own businesses online was that some teachers were already working online. I spent a lot of time studying and researching what was already in the marketplace. And the biggest mistake, or the mistake I saw repeatedly, was everybody looked the same. None of the teachers I saw could effectively communicate who they helped, how they helped their students, and what benefit they were going to bring to the student's life.

During the pandemic, more and more teachers realized that online learning was a thing, and they could quickly match their salary by teaching just a few hours a week online. There was, of course, a flood of teachers who joined the race to build their business online, and it quickly created a price war, and a race to the bottom started. But not if you were able to create what I call a *Signature Tutoring Offer*. I'll talk to you about this throughout this chapter. You see, what happened was everybody was a math or science teacher or everybody was a language tutor or a coding teacher or a guitar teacher. No matter what it was, no matter what subject, everyone had the same offer. It was almost like going to fish in a lake, and everybody was standing there with the same bait trying to catch the same fish. The fish just picks which bait to take.

It was the same for the parents and the students who couldn't tell who were the real experts. *Which tutor should I consider hiring for my child?* Or if it was an adult learner, *Which teacher should I hire for me?* This created a big problem and it created a price war. It became a race to the bottom; whoever could charge the least got the student. And this was a trend that kept happening over and over again, but not for the clients I was working with in the program I launched when I first started working with teachers.

Over time, we've continued to refine this because this is the most important part of growing your business as a teacher online. If you cannot differentiate yourself from every teacher out there, you will never be able to charge premium rates, so you'll never get paid what you deserve. You'll never be able to invest in your business because you're not charging premium rates. You won't be able to hire staff. You won't be able to hire a team around you, so you'll be stuck working in the business and not on it. And not only that, if you are not generating revenue inside of your business frequently enough to pay yourself well enough, it does not allow you to grow the business quickly by using things like paid advertising strategies, which we'll talk about later in the book.

The key is to take what you do and turn it into a Signature Tutoring Offer. I'm going to explain to you exactly how to do that. And what I want to get across here is that a lot of teachers struggled with this mindset shift, that they actually had to charge *more* for their services. It's not being greedy, it's to benefit both the student and you. Because if you charged more, you could create a much better experience, provide better resources, and hire a better team, as I mentioned, which ultimately meant it was a win-win for everybody. If you could provide better resources and a better experience for your students, is their success, and are their results likely to go up? Of course. So there's nothing greedy about charging what it is you're worth. You're an expert. You deserve it.

Let's walk through exactly how to create a Signature Tutoring Offer. I'll also share some examples from some of the clients that I've worked with, some of the teachers that I've worked with who were able to do this effectively, and they started to see a significant difference in not only the number of students they were attracting, but the scale and the speed at which they were able to grow their business.

Let's go through the *Rule of One*. The first thing you need to be able to identify is the easy part. What specific subject do you teach? Now, I also saw an issue here that there were teachers who were good at a lot of subjects; they were good at multiple things. And if they're good at multiple things, that created an issue and a problem when they brought this into the marketplace because they were no longer seen as a specialist. Even though they could help a student with reading or math, it created confusion in the minds of the parents and students, and a confused mind doesn't buy! The parents wanted to see who was a specialist in that specific subject area.

If you can teach multiple subjects, you first need to narrow it down to which one you enjoy the most and which subject you have helped students achieve the best results in. This is the first part. So you're no longer seen as the "general practitioner," who can treat many different "ailments." You're now seen as what I like to call "the chiropractor." If I've got back pain, I'm not going to search for a general practitioner, brain surgeon, or heart surgeon. I want to find a chiropractor, the person who's a specialist in solving back pain. So you've got to get this bit right first.

Next, you need to decide which students within that subject you want to teach. The ones you've got the most experience teaching or the students who need the most help in that specific subject? Where is there more urgency for a student to need help with math in their education timeline? Where is there more urgency for a child to need help with reading throughout their education timeline? So the second part is to get a handle on that.

Here's why this is important. The fastest way to grow your teaching business is through group tutoring. Group tutoring allows you to impact more students and to earn more per class. If you deliver it correctly, it also allows you to get your students better and faster results. It's a win-win for everybody. It means you don't have to sit in front of Zoom all day delivering one-on-one lessons.

Now, if you speak to every single student within the subject, guess who you're going to attract? You're going to attract everybody. So what happens is you may end up attracting a student who's in 12th grade or doing their A-level exams and also a student who's in second grade or at primary school. Unfortunately, these students can't be grouped together, so you're unable to create a group quickly.

So the next stage is to narrow down to a specific grade or age group of students where you feel one of the following: you've got the most experience, you enjoy teaching these students the most, or there's more urgency for the student to want help. Once you pin that down, people pay for results. People who want to pay a low cost for tutoring classes online buy because of how cheap the lesson is. But people will pay you a premium price based on the results you can deliver.

This was a big mindset shift that many teachers I worked with had to make. They had to detach themselves from their old way of thinking of charging per lesson and the new idea that they would be charging based on the result they would get the student. So when they brought their Signature Tutoring Offer to the marketplace, they were painting the picture, the ideal world, the ideal scenario that would ultimately get their ideal students to stick their hand up and say, "Yes, I want that."

When I talk about results, the easiest way is to define something tangible. What type of grade or jump in grades can you help the student achieve? Not confidence, not more enjoyment, but something that can be measured. Once you've identified the result, you will have a higher chance of attracting more students, but you need to take it a step further because that doesn't have enough weight on its own. The student doesn't want to get a 1500 SAT score just to get a certificate with 1500 on it. The parents don't just want to see a two-grade jump in their child's reading level to tell people they did it. They don't want just the music certificate after taking guitar lessons. There's a deeper reason why these students want that grade, or there's a deeper reason why the parents want to see their child reading on grade level.

So this takes us to the next part of our Signature Tutoring Offer, and that's the benefit. How does this result impact the student's life? Not just now, but in the future, in the years to come? What doors does this grade or this result open for the student? What doors does it open for the parents? When you're able to go to that level, the parents and the students now see you as the expert because you're able to help them write their story or paint their picture better than they could ever paint it themselves.

And guess what? You also look different from every other teacher out there who starts to market their offer and just talks about how many lessons they're going to give and what the price is for their service. You now have a solid offer. But there's one more piece to the puzzle that makes it work, which is the key to finalizing your Signature Tutoring Offer. *How do you get the students to that result?* I want you to think about this. When you take an Uber or a taxi, a Lyft, or Bolt, depending on what country you're in, what happens? The taxi map appears on your phone and asks for your location. You put the location in, and then the next thing you do is type in the destination. So far, this is pretty much what we've done with our Signature Tutoring Offer. We've been able to communicate which student we help, what subject they want, where they are right now, what result we're going to get this student, and what the benefit of achieving that result is going to be.

Something is missing, though—the route. Because what happens when you order the Uber or taxi and put in the pick-up location and destination? It immediately shows you how you're going to get there. What this does is give you confidence. It gives you certainty that you will actually end up at the final destination. If the Uber driver says to me, "I don't know how I'm going to get you to your destination," I'm not getting in that Uber. So, this is the key.

We call this a unique learning method. You need to be able to communicate to the parents and the students with your Signature Tutoring Offer the 1-to-5 steps that will help the student get from struggling or from where they currently are in their education to the final destination, where they're able to experience those benefits that you've communicated to them. And when you do this, you go from selling based on features and selling just tutoring lessons to actually having a roadmap and a result that you can now market. If you don't get this right, it's like pouring money into a black hole when you start to market your teaching business. Unfortunately, so many people are failing to get this right. No matter what marketing campaign they launched or the advertising strategy they were using online, without a Signature Tutoring Offer, it was doomed to fail.

A parent or student needs to know you can help them. *Does what you're offering work?* They need to know it will work for them specifically before they're willing to trust you and sign up to work with you. I'll share more on how you go about this later in the book when we talk about how to present a Grand Slam Group offer when you deliver student enrollment calls.

Now I'm going to share with you a story from one of the clients I was working with and still am working with at this particular time. Her name is Quanita. Quanita was an elementary school reading teacher in Texas; she taught reading to the students. And Quanita was really, really good at her job. She loved working with students. It gave her a lot of fulfillment teaching third grade. Now, what happened was Quanita was getting to the point where she was feeling major burnout. Like many teachers, particularly after the pandemic, her schedule completely changed because there were so many demands on her when she returned to the classroom. At the end of the 2021 academic year, she decided enough was enough.

Quanita had already been gaining some experience working with students privately online. Still, she'd struggled to get the traction she wanted and hadn't been able to enroll as many students as she knew she could. The reason was she hadn't positioned herself differently from any of the other reading teachers out there. Being from the United States, where reading is a big thing, Quanita was in a very competitive market. There are a lot of parents who want the best for their children, and they want them to be able to read. It's one of the key core foundational skills. Without being able to read effectively, the student would not be able to learn or develop in any of the other key subjects at school.

We helped Quanita learn to position herself differently from all the other tutors online by identifying her ideal student, what age group they were, what grade in school, and what difference the students would see once they started working with her. Quanita helped students improve two grade levels in their reading in just twelve weeks. So, we added a timestamp on it as well.

From her teaching expertise and experience, we mapped out everything she would do with a struggling reader to create her unique learning method. She was clearly able to communicate: first, we're going to do this, and the next thing you need to do is that. Then it's this, now that, and we took her Signature Tutoring Offer to the marketplace. Twelve weeks later, Quanita generated $50,000 after leaving her teaching position at the beginning of June 2021. And then, the next month, she generated over $45,000 in September 2021.

Quanita was just different. Quanita was "the chiropractor" the parents needed and sought. So when she launched her advertising campaigns, she looked different than everybody else because she had something unique; she had a Signature Tutoring Offer, and parents were willing to pay her based on the results and the benefits she could get for their child. They knew how she would help their child, so she immediately earned trust and demonstrated more value so she could charge what she was worth. Quanita has continued to scale her business successfully.

Chapter Three

The Student Lead Machine

Now that you have a Signature Tutoring Offer in place, this is where things start to get fun. You can now start to advertise your business because you've got the foundations down. You're no longer going to be pouring money into a black hole when you start to market your business and tap into strategies like paid advertising.

That leads me to this. The other issue I saw inside the online teaching space was that teachers were not marketers. Teachers are used to acquiring students through referrals and word of mouth. So now that more teachers wanted to grow their businesses online, not only was there more competition, but the referrals slowed down. And when the referrals slowed down, many tutors were stuck in a cycle: Get students every September at the start of the academic year, have a full schedule, and work with these students until the exams the following year in May and June. These students would then graduate, and it would be time to repeat the process. The teachers would take the summer holidays off because work was light, there weren't many students looking for teaching, and then do it all again. It was like a giant hamster wheel that lacked consistency and predictability.

These teachers lacked the most important skill you will learn as a business owner and as an online tutor—that skill is marketing. It's learning how to advertise and create awareness for your services, for your offer. You will never grow if you cannot acquire clients predictably and consistently. And a plant that doesn't grow does what? It dies. I will starve if I don't know where my next meal is coming from. And if I starve, I die.

As harsh as that may sound, the same is true in business. If you do not have a predictable system to acquire clients, in this case, students consistently, you will go out of business quickly. It's the main reason why businesses fail. But this only works if you have that Signature Tutoring Offer in place.

Now that you understand the importance of the Signature Tutoring Offer, the next step is to build a Student Lead Machine. Let's dive into what the Student Lead Machine is and how it works so that you're set up for success in advertising your business.

Whether you like it or not, you're no longer just a teacher; you're no longer just a tutor. You need to become a digital marketer because the world is now online. The people, the teachers, the tutors, and the business owners who become the best digital marketers will ultimately be the ones who win long term.

I also want to point out that there is no harm in acquiring students through referrals, as it clearly demonstrates you're doing a good job. I think it's important to highlight some other issues with solely relying on referrals to grow your online teaching business. As I said before, they're not consistent. So while referrals are a fantastic way to acquire a student because it means you're doing a good job, you cannot rely on them. And not only that, but if you get referred, it's likely that the student is a different age, has different abilities, and wants help in a different subject. So again, what ends up happening is you start selling your time because students don't come around frequently enough, and you have no choice but to take the student on because you don't know when your next referral is coming. You must open up more calendar space because the students most likely can't be grouped together. Again, you're selling your time instead of creating a model where you can teach one to many.

So what is the fastest way to get students online? The fastest way is paid advertising on social media. Paid advertising on social media gives you predictable lead flow, which is the life and blood of any business. It's the first thing that you need to figure out. Once you know how to get leads, you're able to feed your business. Just like we can walk into the kitchen at home and have food whenever we want. Our business needs to eat whenever it wants.

There are a couple of options. You can spend all day posting on social media, like many of you reading this book may have done. And while you might have had some success, it's not predictable and difficult to track. We spoke about tracking back in the *Five to Thrive*—if you can't measure something, you can't manage it. It's also time consuming. So you're going to pay one way or the other. The time you spend posting on socials never replenishes; you can never get it back. You need to start thinking like a business owner and pay with money instead of time. Money is simply a tool; money replenishes.

We've already learned that people will want to work with you if you have a Signature Tutoring Offer. The beauty of paid advertising is that it allows you to *target* your ideal students, your customers, and clients. It allows you to create awareness from people who want what you've got by placing an advertisement in front of them so that you can communicate your marketing message.

Paid advertising gives you speed. The goal of investing in paid advertising is to make money in return. It's just the faster way of doing it. It's a smarter way of doing it. When I first started to teach this to the clients I was working with the last couple of years, I would see a lot of people try to model us and copy us in the teaching marketplace. The issue was these people did not have a Signature Tutoring Offer, and they were using the wrong strategy. I'll explain.

This might sound counterintuitive, but just because you have an online business does not mean you need a website. A website is confusing. The Student Lead Machine is not a website. The goal of the Student Lead Machine is to take a prospect using a paid advertisement directly from the marketplace to a direct conversation with you as fast as possible in the simplest way possible, eliminating any confusion.

When we saw people try to model what we were doing, they would simply launch similar paid advertisements on social media and copy the same advert our clients were deploying. People would end up on their website and were overwhelmed with information: they'd see an "about you" page—a pricing or services page—a success story or testimonial page, which confused the prospect. They didn't know what to do as there were too many options and too much friction.

Marketing needs to be kept simple. Tutors using this strategy did not create consistent bookings from students and also created competition. They turned potentially ideal clients into window shoppers. Because once prospects have seen one website with so many options, their next move is to go to Google and start researching other tutoring sites to make comparisons. So you're actually preventing potential prospects from having a conversation with you by overcomplicating the process.

Here's how the process should work. You launch an advertisement that details your Signature Tutoring Offer. The next step is to send them to a page where they can only do one simple set of actions: enter their email, their name, and their phone number. Because you've clearly demonstrated and communicated what the offer is, how you're going to help the student, what benefits it will give them, and how you will get them to this result. After the parent or student enters their basic information, you now create an opportunity for them to book an appointment on your calendar to speak with you regarding your services.

Not everybody will initially trust you enough to book an appointment to speak with you. You'll need to build that trust and provide some more value first. Here's what is important. You now have some key information to call and follow up with these prospects because they showed interest, but they just didn't trust you enough yet, or they maybe ran out of time.

I'm going to talk to you about some clients who've been successful with our paid advertising process using our Student Lead Machine. These clients have been able to use paid advertising to take somebody in the marketplace who knew nothing about them and convert them into a student who paid them a few days later.

Let me introduce you to Tutu. Tutu is one of our biggest success stories. She is a former secondary school math teacher from the UK. When I met her, she was a single mom with a huge desire to change how math was taught to today's students.

Back at the start of the pandemic in 2020, Tutu knew she needed a reliable and fast way to enroll students in online tutoring. Her in-person tuition center had to close overnight when the pandemic hit, and she was left with only two students who wanted to continue with her online. The issue she faced was that to get students for her in-person center, she had been posting flyers in people's mailboxes in her local area. These methods weren't sustainable because Tutu was paying with her time by putting out flyers. This had no predictability because she didn't know if her ideal clients were even living at the addresses. She couldn't leave her house anymore because the whole country was in lockdown. Something had to change fast.

The pandemic had broken her business, so she had to rebuild from scratch. After we started working together, Tutu set up our Student Lead Machine. She launched her first paid advertisement, and within three weeks, Tutu was able to enroll 83 new students.

Tutu now had a predictable way to grow her business. She was now able to breathe, and she knew she could move forward quickly because she had something that was consistent. Gone was the fear of not knowing when she was going to receive a phone call from a new parent inquiring about her tutoring services. Things accelerated quickly for Tutu; six months later, those 83 students had grown to 500.

This was at the back end of 2020. So, in December 2020, Tutu went from her business being pretty much wiped off the face of the earth overnight, and being left with two students, to learning how to use paid advertising and building out a Student Lead Machine, and working with 500 students.

Now, because she was able to attract her ideal students so fast by using paid advertising to communicate her Signature Tutoring Offer in the marketplace, she was able to quickly group the students because she was only bringing in students of a similar age and a similar ability.

I've continued to work with Tutu, and she continues to hit milestone after milestone in her business. I remember receiving a message from Tutu in May 2022 saying:

"You've changed my life. My business just brought in £122k cash in a single month. We're now working with 2,000 students in ten different countries around the world. I can't thank you enough." - Tutu

Watching somebody grow, learn this digital marketing skill, and implement it consistently was the best feeling ever. Seeing Tutu grow her business to this level where she is now creating worldwide change has been truly incredible, and she deserves all her success. Think about it. If Tutu, a single mom and former secondary math teacher was posting flyers through people's doors and in their mailboxes to get students, what's stopping you from learning how to advertise your own business and attract your own dream students? The only thing is the process, the strategy, and learning the skill of marketing. Tutu is not smarter than you as an educator. She doesn't have more time than you as an educator, she just has a better process.

There are so many success stories and examples I could give you to show you how important and effective a Student Lead Machine is for your business, but I wanted to highlight Tutu's story to show you what is possible when you get this right. If there's one skill you can learn, it's how to market your business online the right way with the right strategy. You need a Student Lead Machine.

Chapter Four

The Student Acquisition System

How many times have you bought something from a stranger without doing any research? The answer is probably not very often. And the same is true for your tutoring business or, for that matter, anything you would be selling, particularly in an online environment. Because remember, this is not a store or a shop where you meet someone face to face. These prospects that you are now getting awareness from after you've built your Student Lead Machine, are seeing you for the first time. So they have every right to think, *Who the hell is this person that I've just found on the internet? Who is this stranger?* The likelihood that they will immediately book a call with you and the next day jump on Zoom and hand over the money to educate their child—it simply doesn't work like that.

So many people are unsuccessful with their advertising efforts. And so many tutors out there have tried to grow their business by investing in social media advertisements. The first time they speak to somebody and this particular student or parent says, "No, this is not for us," it raises a red flag for tutors who now believe that advertising online doesn't work. But to make the Student Lead Machine successful, you need to build a showroom for your business to quickly establish trust and do the selling upfront. I will share with you in this chapter exactly how to do this.

What I'm about to share is the missing piece of the puzzle for many tutors who have tried but failed to switch to group teaching. Even though they knew it was key to scaling their business, they were stuck because they didn't have this missing marketing piece. No matter how many parents they spoke to, how good they were at teaching or the results that they got previous students, or how good their advertisements were, they still couldn't pivot toward the group model. So if you're at the beginning of your teaching journey, you will be set up for success right from the beginning. If you're a tutor who's previously failed to sell group tutoring online, you'll be given all the tools you need to turn it from failure to success.

Here's a stat for you, 2% to 5% of people buy something the first time they see it. That leaves 95% of people who don't buy. So to increase your conversions with the remaining 95%, you need a Student Acquisition System.

I want you to see your advertising & marketing for your business as two different phases. First is the *Awareness Stage*. Think of this like being a farmer. A farmer goes out and plants seeds in his field. Once he's planted the seeds for that particular season, he now fertilizes the crop. Every day he makes sure these crops are watered, and the seeds grow, and then he harvests them. It's the same for your business. Marketing follows the same steps as the farmer and his crops.

After you have awareness, you move to the *Nurturing Phase*. Let me give you a real-life example: Think about Lamborghini. A Lamborghini has a high perceived value and is seen as a luxury worldwide. We already know the value of a Lamborghini, so there are no questions regarding the price point or the price tag attached to the car. People already value it as a luxury car, which is why a lot of people are willing to do whatever it takes to own and drive the car. They don't care about the cost. They just want to sit in the Lamborghini. They want to drive it out of the showroom because they want the status, benefits, and life they believe the car will give them. They've been marketed to repeatedly by the Lamborghini brand. They didn't just see the car for the first time and then hand over $300,000. No, Lamborghini built its showroom and marketed to these people not once, not twice, but many times until they eventually handed over their hard-earned cash and drove out of the showroom in the car.

When it comes to group tutoring, you need to plant the seeds first and then water them. Your advertisements with your Student Lead Machine are simply the awareness stage. You're buying yourself seeds so that you can fertilize these seeds. And some point down the line, as long as you don't stop marketing to these "seeds" you've gained, they will sprout into students for your business and make you money. Unfortunately, many people stop at the awareness stage and fail to follow up. They fail to keep marketing and demonstrating why the student should work with them.

Why should the student enroll in one of your programs? Think about it this way. You are a tutor who knows group tutoring is the future. Group tutoring gives you more time and allows you to scale your business faster. If delivered correctly, it's the best way to get your students results, hands down. Do your prospects think the same way as you, or do you need to educate them first to help them see these things through new lenses? When students and parents first see an advertisement from you, not everyone is already thinking, *We need a tutor.* The marketplace is divided into three different segments:

1. *The parents and students who are unaware.* They've got no idea that tutoring is even a thing.

2. *The "problem-aware" parents and students.* Parents and students who realize that they need help with their education. But they're not quite sure yet what the solution could be. It could be an online course. It could be a YouTube video. It could be speaking to their teacher at school, maybe it's a tutor, maybe it's an app, or maybe they just need to study harder.

3. *The problem and solution aware.* This is the smallest group. These parents and students are already out there looking for a tutor. They know that a tutor is the answer; they're already looking around, but they don't know yet that group tutoring is the solution. As soon as your Student Lead Machine has collected the contact details from a potential student or parent, you need to start marketing to them.

It's like a conveyor belt. You've taken them through the first stage and they're moving along the conveyor belt to the next stage, where you will educate them, provide value and build trust. You'll start to demonstrate the power of group tutoring, its benefits, and why it's superior to one-on-one lessons.

Now, here's a question for you. Would you rather do the selling upfront so that by the time you jumped on a call with a student or a parent, they already knew what to expect? Do you think that would make it easier to sell your services for group tutoring? Of course, it would make it easier because people are already coming to discuss the benefits with you. So when you do present your offer, and you present the investment to work with you, there's no sticker shock. This is a really important part; without this, the whole model I'm sharing with you would crumble.

Hopefully, you're beginning to see the big picture and how important each stage that I'm sharing with you is in sequential order.

Let me walk you through what this Student Acquisition System looks like and how you avoid objections rather than having to handle them. How do you build a conversion mechanism that builds trust with the parents and students so that by the time you speak to them, they no longer see you as a stranger they saw on the internet the day before? Instead, they're excited to speak to you. They already want to work with you, and all that's left for you to do is seal the deal and show exactly what it would look like for the student if they signed up to work with you. Let's get into it.

You may have heard of a marketing term called the Rule of Seven. It states, on average, a prospect needs to see or hear from you seven times before they make a purchase. And while it is generally true that a prospect will need to see you multiple times before they move forward, many experts believe this magic number seven has doubled because right now, people are marketed to so frequently online their "scam alert" barriers are stronger.

More and more advertisers have moved online and are tapping into the power of social media marketing, which means there's a battle for the attention of your potential students. So with that in mind, let's walk through how to build a Student Acquisition System for your business so you can get more students for group tutoring.

Your Student Acquisition System needs to communicate three things:

1. Your unique learning method and strategy for your students.
2. The importance of a winning environment.
3. Building successful study habits.

These three elements make up what I call *The Learning Trifecta*. When you can communicate these three things effectively, it positions you as the expert for your services.

Now, there's a big mistake I've seen tutors make when they've tried to imitate our successful system. They think, *Ah, it's going to be as simple as copying what they're doing, and this will work for me too.* But there are many things behind the scenes that make this Student Acquisition System convert, which I will share.

You are not selling a product. Your job is to become a "problem solver" and not a "product pusher." Let's dive into the first step of the learning trifecta. I'll also be going into more detail about this in later chapters.

The first part of the learning trifecta is *The Strategy*. What is your unique strategy for getting the student from A to B, your unique learning method? As we discussed earlier in the book, what are the turns in the road when thinking of it like ordering an Uber? Parents and students need to know every turn they're going to make, which gives them confidence, trust, and certainty that you can actually help them. So this is one of the things that you need to share.

You need to get into more depth about what it would look like if you did work together. But keep in mind there is a fine line. Your goal is to explain and teach the "what" and not the "how." The "how" comes when they decide to work with you. So that's the first part of the trifecta.

The second part is *The Environment*. The environment of being in a group versus one-on-one. The difference between the lone wolf who always dies as opposed to being in the tribe that always survives. You want to explain the benefits of being on a team, around other people who want the same thing as you, so when you present to the group on the call, when you speak to a student and parent, they get it. They understand you've already started to influence them and change their perception. You've already started to turn this person into the perfect student. What would that be like? Imagine jumping on a call with somebody who was already your ideal student and bought into your methods.

The last piece of the trifecta is *Building Successful Study Habits*. You need to share with the parent and student why they haven't been successful prior to working with you. It's not because they're not capable; they just haven't built the right habits. They haven't become the student who is working as hard as other students who are achieving the grades they want to achieve. So building these habits, this brand new operating system, so that you are no longer selling just the product, you are selling a new identity to the student. This now puts you head and shoulders above everybody marketing their services online. As a teacher, they now see you as different. They now see you as the go-to tutor, the expert, and they can't wait to speak to you.

Now, here's how the Student Acquisition System works. This is something you would present to your prospects after they book an appointment to speak with you. It could be delivered as a resource, as a written document, or as a short video training. You set this as an initial homework task for the new parents and students to complete before your first conversation on Zoom or over the phone. This works well because your students are already used to completing homework. So before joining the call, they've been given something of value from you, and you are already conditioning them to become great students if you end up working together.

Here's a line I read from motivational speaker and self-development author Brian Tracy. He says, "Approach each customer with the idea of helping him or her solve a problem or achieve a goal, not of selling a product or service." And that's exactly what you're doing here. You're helping them understand how you can solve their problem. So now you've gained that trust that we spoke about.

Let's also consider that you speak to a parent or a student on a call. And for some reason, whatever it may be, it's not the right time to work together. Maybe they can't afford to work with you, which is quite possible. Maybe they just weren't ready yet. Maybe they weren't quite the right student. Maybe there just wasn't enough trust. Whatever the reason this prospect didn't end up becoming a paid client initially, you now have a student on your conveyor belt. Just because you didn't work with the student the first time around, you're going to continue to market to them using the advertisements in your Student Lead Machine.

Remember the *Rule of Seven*? This is where it comes into play. The student and a parent will transition from the "I'm not ready" stage to "how can I start" because they continue to see this same video training, or resource over and over. And the more they see it, the more sense it makes. They see what you have to offer a few more times in your marketing follow-up methods. Remember, the fortune is in the follow-up.

You're going to use things like email marketing and retargeting advertisements, which is just paying for advertisements to be positioned in front of parents and students who've already heard of you. This is a cheap way of advertising because you are speaking to a warmer audience.

When these parents and students keep seeing you, eventually, they'll be ready to get started. Remember, I said you need to become a farmer.

You need to plant seeds by generating leads, and then you need to fertilize and water those seeds by following up with them. Before speaking to a parent or student, you must give them homework. The homework shows them a quick introduction, that you understand them, and demonstrates your unique method. You explain and talk about the learning trifecta and you plant the seed of group tutoring. This is the key. This is the missing marketing piece of the jigsaw puzzle we spoke about.

Now, this isn't easy. This is a really hard skill. So I built the entire Student Acquisition System resource to make things easier for my clients to plug it into their business and use it as homework for their students. I created everything from the years of experience I gained through learning how to market my own businesses online.

As soon as I gave this to the teachers, they were immediately able to use it successfully. There was no guesswork. They had a proven framework. And to be honest with you, this has helped us at The Teacher Project continue to get our clients amazing results. It's what allowed us to go from zero to $3 million in revenue in just two years because results are everything. The more results that you get, the more clients you get. It's the same for you in your business. This one piece saved so much wasted money for our clients marketing their tutoring business online and shortened their learning curve. It shaved so much wasted time off of what the clients needed to do, and it set them up for success right from the beginning, just like one of our clients, Doulton.

Doulton had been following us for quite a few months before she became a client. She was in my Student Acquisition System.

Doulton started as a seed I'd gained through my awareness stage, my lead machine. Doulton wasn't initially ready to work with us; she had a phone call with us, but she wasn't quite ready. The trust wasn't quite there, so she didn't enroll with us initially. However, she stayed inside the Student Acquisition System and continually saw the content we were producing and our training material. Eventually, she moved from the "I'm not ready" bucket to the next bucket of "how can I start."

Doulton experienced it firsthand in our acquisition system, and eventually, she became a client. I do want to point out that Doulton already had a successful business. She'd already taken her tutoring business from zero to seven figures online. She'd done extremely well and gained a lot of experience working in the online tutoring space.

What Doulton was looking for now was the 'edge' to stay ahead of the competition and improve her student acquisition strategies to continue to scale her business because when the pandemic hit, Doulton, just like Tutu I spoke about earlier, found it hard to either keep students or gain new students consistently at the speed she was doing pre-pandemic—the marketplace had changed. When the first academic year ended after the pandemic, Doulton didn't know if she would reopen her business that following September. Super scary. But what Doulton wanted was something that could re-position her offer as premium to her ideal students and allow her to demonstrate the value she could bring to them if they worked together. More and more tutors had gone online, and it became more competitive for existing tutoring businesses like Doulton's. She needed to set herself apart from the crowd and show that she had the experience and was the true expert.

We helped Doulton integrate the Student Acquisition System into her business whilst improving her current marketing strategies, and guess what happened. Ten months later, she had generated more than a million dollars for her business. Doulton continued to implement these strategies and continued to build her follow-up system combined with her new Student Lead Machine, so she had more predictability to be able to scale her business like she was doing pre-pandemic. She had a new way of demonstrating that she was the leader in the marketplace and the true expert. So when parents and students came across her, the selling part had pretty much already been done. They already knew that they wanted to work with her because she had gained trust. She demonstrated value, and she'd shown the parents and students how she was going to help them, not just what she was going to give them.

So wind the clocks forward, and Doulton had her most successful month ever. She generated more than $500,000 in a single month tutoring online. If Doulton can do it, who says you can't? And yes, as I mentioned previously, Doulton already had a successful business, but sometimes the small hinges swing the big doors. You're just one or two pieces away from that next level of success, whether you're starting at the bottom of your business or a little bit further along like Doulton was.

Chapter Five

The Grand Slam Group Offer

Hate sales? When you learn what I'm about to share with you in this chapter, it might just become your favorite thing to do. I'm serious, so stick with me.

One of the things I quickly realized was teachers weren't very good salespeople. When it came to making a sale involving money, it became awkward and uncomfortable for many teachers. They had never needed to jump on the phone and sell their services. The students came to the school. The only selling that the teachers had to do was to sell the students on doing the work, which, if they were able to control the classroom, was a pretty easy thing to do. But when it comes to selling yourself, which is what you're ultimately doing, when it's a transaction that involves the exchange of money, it's an entirely different ballgame.

When I first launched The Teacher Project, there were a lot of teachers who responded to my ads and filled my calendar. I was speaking to teachers all day long, and all of them said the same thing, "Every parent I speak to, or every student that I speak to, they want to work with me. I have a 100% close rate. Just give me the leads and get me on a call with prospective students and their parents, and they'll enroll, no problem."

I'd follow up and ask, "Where did these students come from?" And, you got it, they were referrals.

Now, let's be honest. Selling your services to a referral is easy. They've already made the buying decision in their mind. They're just sitting on the other end of the phone or on Zoom thinking, *Yeah, we've already made our decision. We'll let you go through your sales presentation because we don't want to be rude*, but ultimately they are already going to join your services. So there were a lot of teachers that thought they had a 100% close rate, but they'd only built their business through word of mouth or referrals. So, of course, once these teachers started to actually sell to prospects who didn't know them, to strangers, they started to see it wasn't that easy. They realized that they lacked a few different skill sets.

Now, along with learning how to advertise and market your business, I really believe that learning how to sell is one of the most important skills you'll ever learn in life. When you learn how to sell correctly, you are helping the person you speak to make the best possible decision for themselves. You're not one of these used car salesmen trying to sell something to somebody they might not necessarily believe in. You're a teacher who's going to change this student's life. So it's your job to communicate that to them effectively. There are only a few ways to actually do it and present what you have to offer in the right way so that the students say yes. And remember, we're no longer selling one-on-one tutoring at this point. We're now selling group tutoring. You're now trying to sell your services at premium rates. There may be other teachers out there trying to undercut you with extremely low rates, pretty much giving away tutoring because they believe that education should be free and in a school setting. But when you've got your own business, you can't give away free lessons and trials because your business sales are like food for your body. Without sales, the business is going to die. So it's your job to learn how to sell, and lucky for you, you're going to learn how to do it correctly.

Let me tell you a story about my journey in sales. I've already shared how I learned to sell my personal training services. I also learned how to sell my online fitness coaching to teachers. So when I started selling my services to the tutors, many of them said yes. It felt extremely easy. But when I first started working with the initial 50 tutors, this was my validation period to make sure what I had actually worked, and the fee I charged was much lower. That validation period didn't last long as I began to see the incredible, life-changing results my clients were getting. I was ready to raise my rates to reflect that value and charge what I knew I was worth. I started to see some of my own roadblocks. I got exposed because my sales skills weren't as strong as I thought. When you want to charge premium rates, sales skills are everything.

Now, it would have been easy to say I had bad leads or my prospects didn't have money, but I didn't. The only thing I changed was learning how to sell because I knew if I could do that, I could fix my entire business. So I set out on a mission to upgrade my sales skills, knowing it would benefit me and help my clients grow their own teaching businesses, help them sharpen their own sword, so to speak. I began a three-month mission and hired a sales mentor.

After those three months, I saw my close rate on the calls climb from around 18%, slowly up to 40%, then up to 53%. When I took my last call in April of 2021, I had closed 64% of the sales during that month. Here's the interesting thing. I didn't change my marketing. The leads were still the same. I just changed my sales skill set.

After experiencing those results, guess what I did? I took everything I had learned from working with some of the best sales mentors in the world and molded it for my clients: the teachers and the tutors. I created what I now call *The Grand Slam Group Offer*. The results were incredible because, let's also be honest, education is different. Education isn't like selling fitness or other generic products or online courses online. Education always involves more than one person. There are the parents and the student. So you need to influence and help the people you're speaking with to make a collective decision. Plus, when selling our services to students, we have to make sure that we do it empathetically and passionately. We need to make sure that we focus on why the student needs help, what's in it for them, and how it will benefit them. So I had to tailor how we did this.

The Grand Slam Group Offer was a complete game changer to the sales process. The tutors I was working with saw their results skyrocket. I was working with teachers who were initially selling their services for $800, and they immediately raised their rates to $3,000+ to provide a better experience for their students. I'll give you some examples later.

Here's how you become great at sales, and here's what you need to keep in mind the next time you deliver your next consultation with a new student and parent.

Rule number one, don't be the personal trainer. Back when I transitioned into personal training after my final teaching position in London, I saw a lot of other trainers selling a basic diet plan and a few workout sessions and expecting their clients to pay them a premium rate. Let's be honest, people aren't going to pay very much for a diet plan and a workout because you can get them on Google and YouTube for free. So this is rule number one: You need to actually have something of value to present. You are no longer just selling tutoring lessons. No, you need a Grand Slam Group offer.

So here's how you deliver your next consultation. The first thing you're going to do is learn about the student. This is something you might be doing anyway. You need to understand what they want help with and if you can help them. What are their struggles? What are their main challenges? What are their frustrations? So you can actually formulate a personalized plan. It's no good offering a one size fits all cookie-cutter approach to help students improve their education. Before you present your tailored offer, you must uncover key information about the student's current situation. Once you've done that, the offer is broken down into three stages.

Stage one is to remind them of the seed you planted in your acquisition system, the learning trifecta. Remember, people's attention span is limited. Just because you've said it once, don't expect that this is all you need to make the sale. I said you'll do most of the setting up front. Now you've got to get the parent and the student to cross the line. So what you also need to do is bring this back into the consultation to remind them when they say, "Yes, I remember that." They need to be reconnected to what you've already shown them prior to the call for it to be effective.

So the first thing you do after you've learned about the student is you present two parts of the learning trifecta to highlight the importance of *a winning environment* and *building successful habits* to make the strategic plan you're about to create for the student successful. Once that's been accomplished, you can walk the parents and the students through the strategic plan to help them. This is essentially your unique learning method from your Signature Tutoring Offer, and you tailor it to the student based on how it will help them solve their problems.

As you walk the parents and students through each step of your method, you will need to ask them specific questions. For example, *How could this help you? Do you believe it would help you?* And you need to make sure they answer with a confident yes. Once you've presented your unique learning method and you've tailored this to the student's journey to enhance their learning, they're now at a point where they want what you have. They can see the roadmap, and they can see how you're going to help them achieve their result. They see you as the expert. You've given them that Uber map.

The last thing you share with them is what we call the deliverables. Here are the tools they're going to get so they can implement this plan. This is the point on the call that you share with the parent and the student your offer in terms of the delivery, how many lessons, how many check-ins, and assessments, and you walk them through this list. In truth, if your plan is presented correctly, then the actual tools and deliverables should be irrelevant. This is where most tutors fail when it comes to sales—they just sell the tools.

Finally, you walk through the investment with the parent and student, and if you've delivered everything correctly, they will be in a much better position to say yes.

I'm going to swoop back around to give you more insight into how you present to the group when you reconnect them to the importance of having a winning environment because, of course, that's the hard part. When these parents and students first reached out, they probably had every intention of looking for a private tutor. You planted the seed in your Student Acquisition System, but how will you make sure that you don't run the marathon and then trip before the finish line? Simple, there's a little story I told my clients about how to sell to the group.

Here's what I would get them to share with the parents and the students: a story about climbing up Mount Everest. You can also test this on your next call, and you can thank me later. Here's how it goes:

"I want you to imagine this. If you were to go on a hike up Mount Everest and climb to the top, would you be more successful if you went on your own? Or if you went with a group of students who wanted to get to the top of that same mountain, which option do you think would give you a higher chance of succeeding? Option one. You go on your own. You rely on your own motivation that's got you to where you are now, needing help. Or option two, we can get you with a group of other students who will be highly motivated and who want to get to the top of that same mountain peak. Which option do you think would make the most sense here?"

Nine times out of ten, they're going to say, "Go with the group." So now, when you let them know that it's a few group lessons per week, they're inclined to want to move forward.

Sales is ultimately about helping people make the right decision and not being like the personal trainer that doesn't challenge their clients by having them pick up the same small weights when their client needs an increase in intensity.

It's normal to see some objections from parents and students, and it's your job to address them when they come up. There will also be times when the parents and the students aren't quite 100% confident in the plan you've presented. So, the next thing is learning how to deal with these objections in a way where you're able to challenge them and guide them and help them so that you jump off the call and know that you did everything in your power to help that student make the right decision. And that is, of course, to work with you.

Get excited about dealing with objections because that's your opportunity to turn a student who's just met you or been following you into your ideal student. If you don't set expectations here, guess what happens? You enroll students who don't do the work. You enroll students who don't submit their homework or get their assignments in on time. And ultimately, if you're trying to build a group tutoring business, the community and environment we just spoke about are everything. You don't want somebody to sink the ship. So making sure you deliver this part and challenging them is key to bringing the right students into your business. Remember, you're in control. You get to choose who you want to work with. It's your business, not the other way around. When you're in a school setting, you don't get to choose who's in your class; you're given students to teach. You're teaching on your own terms now.

When you learn how to sell effectively, you will always know how to make money because your business depends on it, your family depends on it, and so do your students. When you deliver sales calls effectively, your students will be set up for success because they will be more motivated, have higher levels of commitment, and have more respect for you as their leader. Therefore they're more likely to go ahead and get the results that you know you can help them achieve.

I was able to use these exact same skills to build my own sales team. I haven't done a sales call since April 2021, and it's unlikely I'll ever need to do one again. I have been able to transfer these skills to my team and clients, and if I can do it, so can you. Let me walk you through some of the results I've seen some of the tutors I've worked with get in their business.

I'd like to introduce you to a tutor named Kyle. Kyle first came to me burnt out, teaching 25 to 30 hours weekly, doing one-on-one lessons on Zoom. He had students of all different ages, a few different subjects, and he was charging low rates. He'd been making around $5,000 monthly for a few months. Kyle was fairly pleased with where he was, but he had to work too hard for it. He also couldn't scale his business because he was stuck delivering 25 to 30 hours a week. Kyle was tired, and his personal life suffered. He didn't spend any time with his partner, and she kept asking him when things would change.

Well, things *did* change when Kyle started working with me. We helped him switch his offer from a one-on-one to a group-based model by showing him how to market his business and position himself as the go-to tutor so he could attract students who could be grouped together. Kyle learned the art of selling and built a Grand Slam Group offer, which meant that he could go from charging a few hundred bucks per student to more than $2,000 in just a few weeks. Kyle started to see how powerful the art of selling really was.

He started to gain confidence. And I remember getting one message from Kyle that said, *Elliot, you've changed my life. I just hit my first ever $15,000 month. I can't believe how things have changed for me.* Then there's Lori.

Lori was just like Kyle, a tutor selling her services one-on-one, and she'd also started running her first groups again. Lori had the issue of charging $800 for just a few weeks of tutoring. Now, this might have been more than other tutors, but Lori couldn't hit her business and revenue goals. It was very difficult for her to pay her staff and still generate the profit she needed to continue expanding. She wasn't able to invest in marketing, so her business was growing slowly. Lori learned how to sell with the Grand Slam Group offer, and Lori was able to raise her rates from $800 to $3,500!

Over the next year, Lori hit her first $500,000 year, completely changing her business. How? She was able to upgrade the resources and services she provided to her students because she was charging a higher rate. In turn, she helped her students get better results, which meant she had more testimonials to use in her marketing which attracted new students. She was able to pay her staff better and, of course, live a much better quality of life.

Many more teachers have used my Grand Slam Group offer to raise their rates and get paid what they truly deserve by learning how to sell and helping students make the right decision to invest in their education. So I encourage you, don't be scared of sales when you learn how to do it properly, it will become your best friend.

Chapter Six

The Scalable Delivery System

We're almost there. You've learned how to get students with a proven system. But now there's one very important thing left… You've got to help these students crush it.

Remember, results is sales. Having a bucket with a hole in it is no good when you're enrolling students consistently into your business. Because you've been able to position yourself as the go-to tutor, you've mastered the art of advertising, and you've mastered the art of selling. Now you've got to back it all up with results. But here's the good thing about results: the more results you get, the easier it is to sell. You need to go all in on this, which I'm sure you would do as a teacher because you're passionate about helping your students. You need to help your students crush it. The more energy and effort you put into your group tutoring programs, the more longevity your business will have. Your students win, and you'll have more testimonials, more case studies, and more results to send back into the marketplace. This is everything.

In this chapter, I'm going to walk you through the dos and don'ts when building a scalable delivery system, and by that, I mean group tutoring; it's only group tutoring that's scalable. We've already learned that the one-on-one model is not a good long-term solution for students because you're turning them into lone wolves. You're training them to operate solo instead of building them into leaders who will drive our generations forwards.

Why is group tutoring good for you? Well, you already know that. We've talked about how it allows you to teach more students so that you can have more impact. It allows you to earn more per class to provide better resources for your students, which in turn helps them get better results. It allows you to invest more into paid advertising and growth methods so your business can scale. And it also allows you to build a team around you.

I used to get the question from successful tutoring business owners, "I've got a lot of teachers already working with me. Why should I pivot towards a group model when I could just provide the tutor to teach one-on-one?" Well, guess what? It's very hard to manage a tutor delivering so many different lessons. Remember, the whole goal here is to ensure that everybody is benefiting. So if you're the business owner and you're loading your teachers' schedules up with one-on-one lessons, not only are you making things not fun for them, but you're going to burn them out. You're going to make their life more stressful instead of helping them deliver to groups and impact more students, which is what they want to do. They could also earn more because you could afford to pay them more. And when you learn how to deliver the scalable delivery system effectively, the students will also win.

Let me walk you through our model. I'll kick things off with some of the biggest mistakes I've seen tutors make when building their group tutoring model. Mistake number one: The first thing teachers would do when they came to us is they thought that they needed to build their entire tutoring program from the ground up before they could actually market their business. They wanted to build the house before they had any buyers.

This is madness. How often have you seen a housing developer or a real estate developer build a bunch of houses first and then try to sell them? It doesn't happen. They're smarter than that. They create an outline, an image, and a vision of what the house will look like. They make sure they can sell the house, and then they get to work and build.

This is why I've left this to the final chapter. This is the last thing that you need to do. If you're just starting from ground zero, I will save you a ton of wasted time and money. Because the truth is you've already got the teaching expertise and know-how in your mind. You already know how to help students. You don't have to build out the perfect delivery program, fulfillment system, or online course for your students before you have any—you just need to start teaching them. If you're good at what you do, they will get results. Don't build the house before you've sold it. At the beginning of your journey, your only goal is to focus on recruiting students.

Now that that's out of the way, let's talk about what goes into creating a scalable delivery system that produces life-changing results for your students.

I remember my days as a personal trainer and explained earlier in this book how I went from teaching or working with clients one-on-one in London to working with clients five-to-one. I was charging a higher amount per client for a group session than the other personal trainers were charging a client for a one-on-one session. I was basically earning more than five times per hour than every other trainer. I learned that, yes, it was a lot harder and that I needed to be a lot more focused in the actual session because I still needed to deliver the results for my clients; otherwise, this would never work. It felt uncomfortable initially, and you may also feel that way. It's natural to ask yourself questions like, *What if I can't get my students' results online in a group?* If you're a teacher, you've taught maybe 20, 25, or 30 students in a single class at school. It's no different. You'll still be able to help them. There are just a few slight changes and tweaks that I will walk you through that make all the difference online.

Being present in the classroom allows you to have more influence and control, which cannot be felt on Zoom. So when it comes to a scalable delivery system, if you are just selling Zoom lessons and students are doing one to two lessons each week, and that's it, that's all they get, guess what? *Breaking News!*—they will not stay with you very long in your group classes.

You need to create value away from these group classes. That's what I managed to do when I was doing personal training. I realized that my clients weren't just coming to their weekly training sessions for the session itself. They were coming for more than that. They were coming because of the community I had been able to build. I'd been able to facilitate a growth environment where they could all flourish and where they could all push one another in a fun way. I also gave them things to do away from our training sessions, just like when you give your students homework. So not only were they valuing the training sessions with me, they were valuing the community. They valued my expertise and guidance outside of the lessons. They had built friendships with my other clients who had similar goals, and they didn't want to leave that behind because people want connection.

I created a weekly drop-in class, so in addition to their small group sessions with me during the week, one extra time per week, we all met in a larger group. I had all of my clients there, and sometimes there'd be 30 clients who would turn up almost like a boot camp, and we'd go for brunch. It was fun, and people made friends. But this session was purely designed to accelerate their results. If they couldn't make their session that week, they had this additional session to fall back on, and my clients' results were amazing.

When I took this model online, I thought, *If I take some of the things that I'd learned that allowed me to get my clients in that environment better results than I was getting them one-on-one, I wonder if it would work for teachers' teaching groups?* And it did.

I started to map this out. I started to teach the tutors I was initially working with exactly how to do this. I identified six things they needed in their online group tutoring business to make the model work, so the students and the parents knew they were not just turning up for Zoom lessons. Because if all you give your students is Zoom lessons, not only do they not place a high value on this, but when the economy changes, people look at their monthly expenses, realize all you're offering them is a Zoom lesson, and they're more likely to cancel their sessions with you. When you add everything else in, they value everything else more. I guarantee they'll stay with you for longer, and your retention will be higher, just like it's been for my clients.

Here's everything you need: The first thing is *a core curriculum* where you can put all of your knowledge onto an online platform used for self-study. This gives the student or parents a way to learn away from the lessons they attend to enhance what you are teaching them. They have a place to direct them to so they can study and accomplish the work you give them. You can also store recorded lessons a student may have missed for them to access. It also allows you to make your process interactive. It allows you to make it fun with challenges, with worksheets, so if the student needs something, it encourages them to continue learning outside of their lessons.

Remember, you only need to build or create something once you have students. It will be an addition that you include as you go based on your knowledge and your expertise. Long term, once you've worked with your initial groups, you'll have this amazing curriculum for your tutoring offer that every student will get access to. This creates the *"Wow!"* factor.

The next thing to consider in your delivery system is *the number of weekly lessons you provide to your students.* We've found a sweet spot to have two group lessons per week. Think about it, the more you can get in front of a student, the more you can help them and serve them. If you only see somebody once a week, you don't really get them to see much progress. You don't ingrain in them how important it is to actually focus and study; when you see them more, it becomes a habit. They start to enjoy learning more, and when people enjoy something, they get good at it. Again, we've found two group lessons a week is ideal. I've seen tutors deliver more, but honestly, two is the sweet spot. You can see more students in less time and not sacrifice results.

The third component is *building a community component* to create a winning environment, as I did for my clients in London. If you are working with younger students, you could build a community for the parents interested and engaged in their child's education where they could go and communicate with other parents. This could be in the form of an online community group on a social media platform or even just a WhatsApp group; there are many different ways that you could build this. This is vital to building your business because it allows you to internally market to your clients, lead and share your learnings and guidance. Your students or the parents will see you in this community as more than just a teacher. You become a leader, communicating with them and helping them become the perfect student or parent that got their kids to do the work. Over time, your clients facilitate this community for you. This is where the group model becomes really powerful.

The fourth component of a successful online group tutoring business is to have *a weekly drop-in or a catch-up class.* As you develop your group model, there will be times when students need more of a push and more time with you, or maybe they missed a class one week. This extra session allows them to catch-up or get that extra time they need with you. This can be open to everybody: Students who are struggling, or just an opportunity to answer questions so nobody gets left behind.

This next component is where you can really start adding massive value for your students. We've found that *strategically placed one-on-one sessions* with your students during the time frame you work with them make the process perfect. You are essentially building a hybrid model, where they mainly attend the groups, but you identify your students' peaks when they feel awesome and the valleys in their journey when they need more intervention or motivation. You would pick one to three points in a student's journey when they work with you and place these one-on-one sessions: This might be to report back on an exam, review their work, or even assess them. This allows you to leverage your time, and you're giving the student the best of both worlds, and you can only guess what happens when you present all of this in your sales offer to the parent and the student. You've given them more value than any other tutors have offered or presented to them.

The sixth and final component is to back it up with *a world-class support system*. Because now you have the foundations in place to grow, you can build a team to deliver the support for you. You're not running around pouring from an empty cup, fighting fires, or putting out fires, because you've got a group-based model that's set up to deliver the best possible experience for your students to achieve results. These results allow you to continue to market your business and grow in revenue and profit. You can now hire teams to come in and teach these lessons so you can continue to scale and provide world-class support.

Now, there were a lot of teachers I spoke to who were super skeptical of this model. They were stuck in what I call "the dinosaur age," Their mindset was so fixed that the only option was to teach one-on-one because that's what was best; that's how it's always been. Why change it now? Well, not only were they not implementing this scalable delivery system that incorporates my six core delivery components, they hadn't even tried it. When some of the clients I worked with who had been skeptical tried this model, they saw how beneficial it was for their students. One client who comes to mind is Alan from Scotland. He was the typical tutor like Kyle in the previous chapter, delivering about 30 hours weekly with one-on-one sessions. Like most tutors, Alan was stuck in the cycle where he would get to the end of the academic year and lose all of his students because they'd all completed their exams. He'd have the summer off, and it was straight back into the thick of it at the start of each academic year when everybody signed up again. He was stuck delivering one-on-one lessons and not spending time with his family. Alan knew he had to change because he wanted to have more time freedom. He had an online business, but he was glued to his computer. He was not spending time with his family, and his revenue stayed the same because he didn't have the time to market. He then didn't have the time to go and hire another teacher to help him grow. So while Alan was skeptical of this group model and didn't believe in it initially, he knew he had to take the leap of faith, and there was no other option if he really wanted change.

Six months after working together, Alan went from working 35-40 hours a week delivering one-on-one lessons with his revenue stagnant to teaching just four hours a week and earning five times more by implementing my scalable delivery system. He quickly hit his first £10,000 month, and he continued to grow past that to hit £24,000 in a single month for his business. Alan now has a system in place where he sometimes teaches as many as 50 students in a class. He uses this hybrid model, where his students get one-on-one sessions: they get to attend catch-up and weekly drop-in classes. They have curriculums to work with away from Alan and his team.

Alan's been able to employ a student success specialist to keep these students accountable and to give them world-class support to make sure they can thrive. Alan is continuing to grow, working on his business, and no longer being stuck in it in front of Zoom all day. Alan's just one of many examples that I could give you. This really is a game changer when you know how to implement a scalable delivery system effectively so you don't have a hole in the bucket and lose students as you begin to roll out the group model for your business.

Conclusion

So we've about come to the end of our journey together for now. As we wrap up, I want to say I hope you've learned a thing or two that can help you in your journey as a teacher, as an educator, and as someone responsible for building our future generations. I also want to congratulate you on making it this far. Because if you've made it this far, it shows me that you know how important this time is for teachers.

I mentioned it at the start of the book, and I will mention it again. This is the golden era. We don't know if there will ever be another opportunity for teachers to finally get paid what they deserve, impacting more students than they ever thought was possible. Again, remember, the online tutoring space and private tutoring market are growing, but growth doesn't last forever. So if you're with me here, now is the time if you've enjoyed the book. I want to tell you how I can help you at an even greater level.

You might be wondering, *Can The Teacher Project help me?* We help teachers in three different buckets. If one of these fits you, we can help. We help teachers who want to launch their own online business and get it right the first time. Maybe you're still in the classroom, but you want to flourish without the stress and unpredictable workload, doing what you love and getting paid what you feel you deserve. We can help you. Maybe you're the tutor who just wants to find a predictable way to acquire students to hit your first 50 students, 100 students, or first 200 students by switching from a one-on-one to a more scalable delivery model with group tutoring. Maybe that's you.

You may have established a tutoring business that already works with thousands of students. You already have a team of tutors working with you, and you want to scale this to the moon because you know you've got a proven process. You've already helped students crush it, and you really want to take things to the next level. We can help you, too. Here's how we can help and what to do next.

We can show you how to have your ideal students come to you and not your competition and how to fill your inbox with unlimited inquiries using predictable advertising strategies. You'll learn how to build trust with these students by creating a Student Acquisition System, so these students are ready to buy from you before you even speak with them. And then, you'll learn how to present a group Grand Slam Group offer to easily convert these students into paying clients for group tutoring, making sure you can create life-changing results for your students using my six delivery principles for group tutoring so you never need to trade time for money again.

I've left some gifts at the back of this book detailing exactly how you can get started on your journey, whether you're looking to launch, build, or scale.

I look forward to working with you.

Your future Coach,
Elliot

THANK YOU FOR READING MY BOOK!

DOWNLOAD YOUR FREE GIFTS

Just to say thanks for buying and reading my book, I would
like to give you a few free bonus gifts, no strings attached!

To Download Now, Visit:
www.TeachOnYourOwnTerms.com/BookGifts

*I appreciate your interest in my book, and value your feedback as it helps me improve
future versions. I would appreciate it if you could leave your invaluable review on
Amazon.com with your feedback. Thank you!*

Printed in Great Britain
by Amazon

57893100R00047